VINTAGE ART FROM THE ARC[...]

THE NEW YORK PUBLIC LIBRARY

COLORING
IN THE
LIONS

A COLORING BOOK

LINE ART BY
ALEXIS
SEABROOK

HENRY HOLT AND COMPANY · NEW YORK

A New York Public **Library** Book

About The New York Public Library's Digital Collection

In March 2005, The New York Public Library debuted a site called Digital Gallery, which featured 275,000 images from the Library's collections. Since then, the Library has added hundreds of thousands of images to the repository, along with records providing context for the materials.

Over time, the purpose of and need for this site changed. As librarians and staff considered the importance and uses of digitized materials, they came to realize that it was time for the "passive" gallery to evolve. In the summer of 2013, the NYPL Technology Digital Repository Team paired with NYPL Labs to create a sustainable, modern replacement to the decade-old Digital Gallery, and thus Digital Collections was born!

Digital Collections contains 708,100 items and counting. While that's just a fraction of The New York Public Library's overall holdings, the aim of Digital Collections is to provide context for the materials and to inspire people to use and reuse the media and information to advance knowledge and create new works. Spanning a wide range of historical eras, geography, and media, Digital Collections offers drawings, illuminated manuscripts, maps, photographs, posters, prints, rare illustrated books, videos, audio, and more.

The Collection has become a living thing—and it is still growing and changing. In January 2016, the Library released more than 180,000 of its public domain items as high-resolution downloads, available to the public without restriction. Although most items in the release had already been visible at the Library's digital collections portal, the high-quality files are now available for free and immediate download.

The Digital Collections is still just the tip of the iceberg. The Library is working every day to make more of their vast collections easily available to the curious and the creative. Start exploring at publicdomain.nypl.org/pd-visualization.

—————— ஐ ౧౩ ——————

For over a century, the creative and the curious have turned to The New York Public Library for inspiration.

When the Library first opened its doors in 1911, it was inundated with requests for visual materials. To meet the demand, the Library began collecting and organizing images under more than 12,000 different subject headings, and in 1915 the Picture Collection was formed. Today, with so much material available across both the Library and our online Digital Collections, The New York Public Library remains a vital resource for inspiration because the desire and need for visual experience remains.

Libraries have always been a source for information, and people continue to come to the Library to find and learn new things. Whether it's an author or scholar consulting unique historical documents or an artist or designer serendipitously browsing for primary source materials, the process begins at the Library. This research leads to discovery, which leads to inspiration, which leads to creation. Others then discover this newly created work, which starts the process again.

The Library can help you take this same path. You have in your hands a coloring book of images culled from collections across The New York Public Library. The color choices are yours. Don't feel that you need to stay within the lines.

Discovery.
Inspiration.
Creation.

You've discovered. Now be inspired and create!

Billy Parrott
Associate Director, Mid-Manhattan Library
The New York Public Library

70706 FRONT FACADE THE NEW YORK PUBLIC LIBRARY, NEW YORK

BLIC LIBRARY

New York. Public library

Main reading room 1911

Construction photograph, Main reading room
circa 1911
New York Public Library Archives, The New York Public Library

Commercial poster, Columbia bicycles
circa 1895
The Miriam and Ira D. Wallach Division of Art, Prints and Photographs:
Art & Architecture Collection, The New York Public Library

THE NOVEL OF NEW YORK and of TO-DAY

DOLLY DILLENBECK

BY JAMES L. FORD

GEO. H. RICHMOND AND Co.   NEW YORK

Book poster, *From Kingdom to Colony*
circa 1895–1911
The Miriam and Ira D. Wallach Division of Art, Prints and Photographs:
Art & Architecture Collection, The New York Public Library

Book poster, *The Martian*
circa 1895–1911
The Miriam and Ira D. Wallach Division of Art, Prints and Photographs:
Art & Architecture Collection, The New York Public Library

IN HAMPTON ROADS

By
CHARLES
EUGENE
BANKS
&
GEORGE
CRAM
COOK

RAND, McNALLY & CO., PUBLISHERS
CHICAGO and NEW YORK

Magazine poster, *International*
circa September 1896
The Miriam and Ira D. Wallach Division of Art, Prints and Photographs:
Art & Architecture Collection, The New York Public Library

Advertising poster, High Life java and mocha coffee
circa 1895–1917
The Miriam and Ira D. Wallach Division of Art, Prints and Photographs:
Art & Architecture Collection, The New York Public Library

SIR RICHARD ESCOMBE

MAX PEMBERTON

HARPER & BROTHERS, PUBLISHERS

CHERRY

BY

Booth Tarkington

Author of "The Gentleman from Indiana"

HARPER & BROTHERS, PUBLISHERS

"Sir Nigel" *The right to print this story in this publication cost* $25,000.00

THIS THRILLING NEW ROMANCE BY

CONAN DOYLE

THE FAMOUS CREATOR OF "SHERLOCK HOLMES"

Book poster, *Sir Nigel*
circa 1895–1911
The Miriam and Ira D. Wallach Division of Art, Prints and Photographs:
Art & Architecture Collection, The New York Public Library

BOOKS IN THE WAR

THE ROMANCE OF LIBRARY WAR SERVICE

BY

THEODORE

WESLEY KOCH

Book cover, *Books in the War: The Romance of Library War Service*
circa 1919
Rare Book Division, The New York Public Library

FOR SALE HERE.

THE BOOKMAN.

Price, 20 Cents.

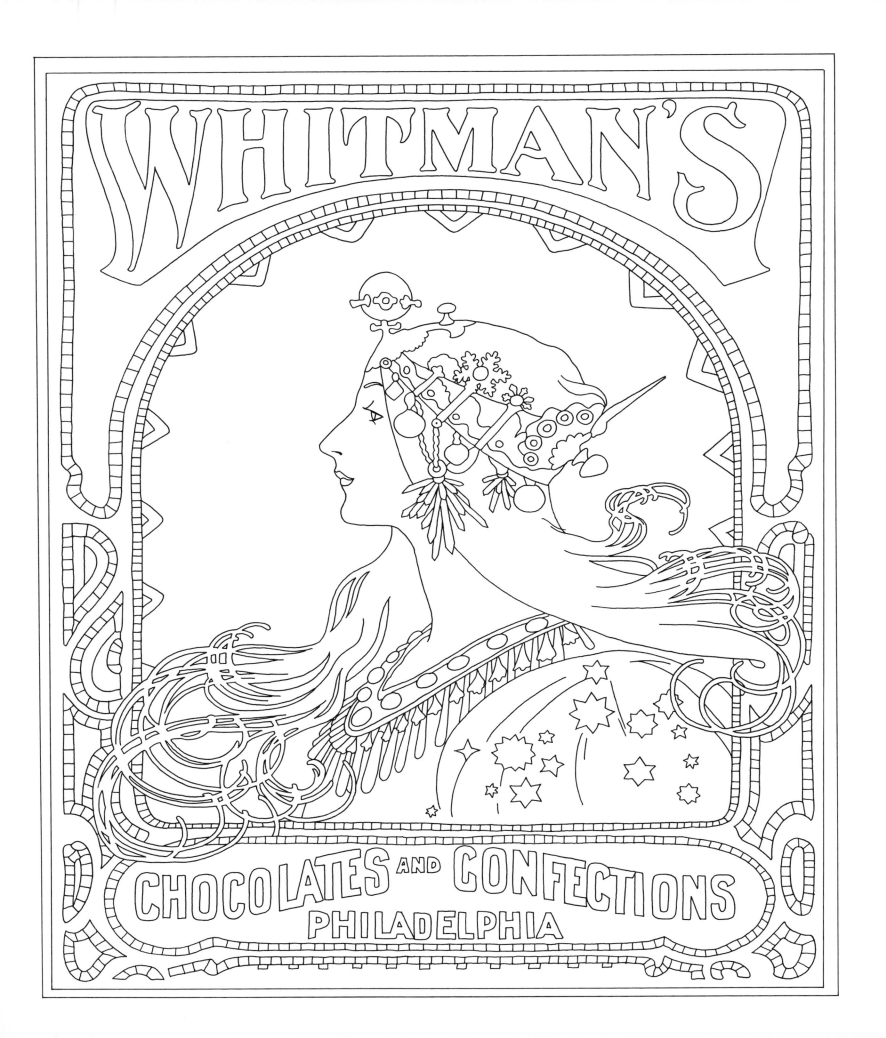

Commercial poster, Whitman's chocolates and confections, Philadelphia
circa 1895–1917
The Miriam and Ira D. Wallach Division of Art, Prints and Photographs:
Art & Architecture Collection, The New York Public Library

Commercial poster, "The Waterbury" Elfin watches
circa 1895–1917
The Miriam and Ira D. Wallach Division of Art, Prints and Photographs:
Art & Architecture Collection, The New York Public Library

Magazine poster, *Dry Goods Economist*
circa 1896
The Miriam and Ira D. Wallach Division of Art, Prints and Photographs:
Art & Architecture Collection, The New York Public Library

Commercial poster, Blue Seal birch beer
circa 1895–1917
The Miriam and Ira D. Wallach Division of Art, Prints and Photographs:
Art & Architecture Collection, The New York Public Library

Commercial poster, D. M. Ferry & Co's standard seeds
circa 1895–1917
The Miriam and Ira D. Wallach Division of Art, Prints and Photographs:
Art & Architecture Collection, The New York Public Library

Commercial poster, Mobile and Ohio R. R. dining cars, Christmas 1902
circa 1902
The Miriam and Ira D. Wallach Division of Art, Prints and Photographs:
Art & Architecture Collection, The New York Public Library

Commercial poster, Feigenspan's bock beer
circa 1895–1917
The Miriam and Ira D. Wallach Division of Art, Prints and Photographs:
Art & Architecture Collection, The New York Public Library

SCHIRMER'S LIBRARY
OF MUSICAL CLASSICS

Book poster, *Schirmer's Library of Musical Classics*
circa 1895–1911
The Miriam and Ira D. Wallach Division of Art, Prints and Photographs:
Art & Architecture Collection, The New York Public Library

Commercial poster, Folies-Bergère, "La Loïe Fuller"
circa 1896–1900
The Jerome Robbins Dance Division, The New York Public Library

Engraving, Melle Ferraris, rôle de Gazella dans l'Etoile de Messine, Théâtre de l'opéra
circa late nineteenth century
Jerome Robbins Dance Division, The New York Public Library

Print depicting Carmencita waltz, Wm. D. Dutton & Co.
circa 1891
Jerome Robbins Dance Division, The New York Public Library

Print depicting Valse chaloupée, "The Apach's dance"
circa 1908
Jerome Robbins Dance Division, The New York Public Library

SHIMMEE BABY

GEORGE WHITE'S
SCANDALS OF 1919

A Modern Musical Revue

Sheet music, "Shimmee Baby," George White's *Scandals of 1919*
circa 1919
Music Division, The New York Public Library

7109. FLAT-IRON BUILDING, NEW YORK.

Print depicting dance, M'elle Caroline Lassia dans Paquita
circa 1846
Jerome Robbins Dance Division, The New York Public Library

GIBSON'S TYPICAL AMERICAN GIRL.

Commercial poster, interior of Grands Express Aériens plane, Paris–London
circa 1922
Science, Industry and Business Library: General Collection, The New York Public Library

MISS PETTICOATS

C. M. CLARK PUBLISHING CO.

Book poster, *Miss Petticoats*
circa 1895–1911
The Miriam and Ira D. Wallach Division of Art, Prints and Photographs:
Art & Architecture Collection, The New York Public Library